# ALL I NEED TO KNOW I LEARNED FROM MY CAT

## (AND THEN SOME)

# ALL I NEED TO KNOW TO KNOW I LEARNED FROM MY CAT

(AND THEN SOME)

By Suzy Becker

WORKMAN PUBLISHING • NEW YORK

Library of Congress Cataloging-in-Publication Data is available.

ISBN-13: 978-0-7611-4766-4

Workman books are available at special discounts when purchased in bulk for premiums and sales promotions as well as for fund-raising or educational use. Special editions or book excerpts can also be created to specification. For details, contact the Special Sales Director at the address below.

Workman Publishing Company, Inc.
225 Varick Street
New York, NY 10014-4381
www.workman.com

Printed in China

First printing: September 2007

10 9 8 7 6 5 4 3 2 1

**ORIGINALLY**

For Amy
and my family. AND BINKY

with special thanks to Ellie, Sally.
Annie and Peter for maki        book
possible. AND BINKY For ev      ¡IDEA
~~In This~~ i'ever hAD.

**AND THEN**

For Lorene
and Edite.

with platinum thanks to Megan. Patrick, Suzie,
Jenn, Irene, Oleg. Amy and Julie and many
fond memories of Sally.

**S**eventeen years ago (a little more than the average cat's life span), ALL I NEED TO KNOW I LEARNED FROM MY CAT introduced the world to the teachings of one not-so-average cat, my cat Binky. The book that you're now holding in your hands, or perhaps resting on your cat's back, commemorates the printing of the >2,000,000th< copy, which is to say, as they do in the music biz, my cat's gone double platinum.

I'm often asked how celebrity affected Binky. Not one to rest on her laurels, she kept right on teaching. By the time she died in 2005 (at the age of 18½), she'd imparted several lifetimes' worth of learning, which I am very pleased to pass on to you, her public. >Forty-five brand-new lessons< (a.k.a. "Volume 1.5") appear in the last third of this book.

**I** have also included, for your use and reuse, a simple screening device, my patented ARE YOU A CAT PERSON? **quiz.** Yes, of course YOU are, but once you learn to administer it properly, my quiz will save you anywhere from hours of unnecessary housecleaning to years of a doomed relationship. Results are generally confirmed within 24 hours.

As I put the finishing touches on this new edition, I was surprised to grieve for Binky all over again. I will never claim to have immortalized her (that would imply she was merely mortal to begin with), but I take great consolation from knowing that she lives on in these pages.

I hope you will, too.

Suzy Becker

BE PEACE.

# ARE YOU
# A CAT PERSON?

MY CAT

| | STRONGLY AGREE | AGREE | DISAGREE |
|---|---|---|---|
| | SA | A | D |
| 1. YOU HAVE MORE PICTURES OF YOUR CATS THAN OF YOUR RELATIVES. | 2 | 1 | 0 |
| 2. YOU REFER TO YOUR CATS as RELATIVES, i.e., THE KIDS, MY GRANDKIDS. | 2 | 1 | 0 |
| 3. YOU HAVE CALLED ANOTHER PERSON BY YOUR CAT'S NAME. | 2 | 1 | 0 |

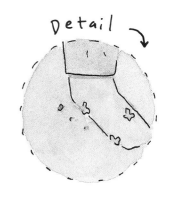

Detail

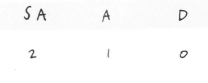

| | SA | A | D |
|---|---|---|---|
| 4. YOU DON'T NOTICE THE CAT HAIR ON YOUR CLOTHES. | 2 | 1 | 0 |
| 5. YOU DON'T NOTICE THE CAT FOOD ON YOUR SOCKS. | 2 | 1 | 0 |
| 6. YOU GO THROUGH THESE LIKE TOILET PAPER. | 2 | 1 | 0 |

|  | SA | A | D |
|---|---|---|---|
| 7. YOU BOUGHT YOUR FURNITURE TO GO WITH YOUR CAT. | 2 | 1 | 0 |
| 8. YOU OWN YOUR FURNITURE. | 0 | 1 | 2 |
| 9. YOU OWN YOUR CAT. | 0 | 1 | 2 |

|  | SA | A | D |
|---|---|---|---|
| 10. YOU CANNOT HAVE TOO MANY* CATS. | 2 | 1 | 0 |

| | >10 | 5-9 | 1-4 |
|---|---|---|---|
| 11. *(YOUR PERSONAL LIMIT IS ☐☐☐.) | 3 | 2 | 1 |

12. WHEN YOU SEE THIS (→), YOU
(A) STARE; (B) DON'T LOOK TWICE; (C) SMILE;
(D) BALANCE YOUR EGGS ON TOP.

| A | B | C | D |
|---|---|---|---|
| 0 | 1 | 2 | 3 |

YOUR _____ ARE SAFE.
(NOUNS 13-17)

| | AGREE | DISAGREE | STRONGLY DISAGREE |
|---|---|---|---|
| | A | D | S D |
| 13. FLOWERS | 0 | 1 | 2 |
| 14. DOCUMENTS | 0 | 1 | 2 |
| 15. SCREEN DOORS/WINDOWS | 0 | 1 | 2 |
| 16. DRAPES | 0 | 1 | 2 |
| 17. SWEATERS | 0 | 1 | 2 |

| | S A | A | D |
|---|---|---|---|

18. YOU CLEAN YOUR CAT'S BATHROOM MORE OFTEN THAN YOUR OWN.

|  | 2 | 1 | 0 |

19. YOU CAN TELL WHICH ONE IS THE PETRIFIED HAIR BALL.

|  | 2 | 1 | 0 |

THERE IS NOTHING WRONG WITH THESE PICTURES:

21.

20.

22.

| | S A | A | D |
|---|---|---|---|
| | 2 | 1 | 0 |
| | 2 | 1 | 0 |
| | 2 | 1 | 0 |

| | SA | A | D |
|---|---|---|---|
| 23. YOU KNOW HOW MANY TIMES IS TOO MANY TIMES TO PAT A CAT. | 2 | 1 | 0 |
| 24. YOU BEAR SCARS FROM PAST RELATIONSHIPS. | 2 | 1 | 0 |
| 25. YOU DON'T TALK TO YOURSELF. (YOU TALK TO YOUR CAT.) | 2 | 1 | 0 |

26. THIS IS YOUR COPY OF THIS BOOK. → 1
THIS IS JUST ONE OF YOUR COPIES. → 2
YOU BORROWED THIS COPY TO SAVE
$9 FOR EXTRA-PREMIUM CATNIP. → 3

 NOW, GO BACK and ADD UP YOUR POINTS
TO DETERMINE YOUR OFFICIAL RATING.

OFFICIAL RATING

CONGRATULATIONS,

1-14 YOU like
CATS!

15-29 You're a
CAT PERSON!

30-51 You're a
CAT FANATIC!

52-55 Please
see a VET!

56 or Check
more your MATH!

# ALL I NEED TO KNOW I LEARNED FROM MY CAT

### (The Original)

MY CAT

IT'S O.K. TO WEAR THE SAME THING EVERY DAY.

SLEEPING IS VERY UNDERRATED

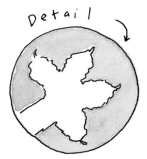

Detail

Never crack
your knuckles.

SO IS STRETCHING.

GROOMING REQUIRES A SERIOUS TIME COMMITMENT.

REMEMBER TO WASH
BEHIND YOUR EARS,

IN BETWEEN YOUR TOES

AND UNDER YOUR ARMS.

KEEP YOUR NAILS TRIMMED,

NOTE: While the public
generally appreciate
good grooming —
they do n<u>o</u>t generally
appreciate it in public.

AND YOUR HAIR CLEAN.

PEE WITHOUT GETTING
ANY ON YOUR SHOES.

GET SOMEONE ELSE TO CLEAN YOUR BATHROOM.

EAT WHEN YOU'RE HUNGRY.

WHEN YOU'RE NOT HUNGRY, PLAY WITH YOUR FOOD.

IF YOU DON'T SEE IT, ASK FOR IT.

HAVE NO QUALMS ABOUT
SHARING A PLATE

OR EATING LEFTOVERS.

DON'T BURP IN PUBLIC.

DRINK MILK.

Try not to obsess about cholesterol.

HELP WITH THE CROSSWORD.

BE HARD TO LEAVE.

NOTICE
THE SQUIRRELS.

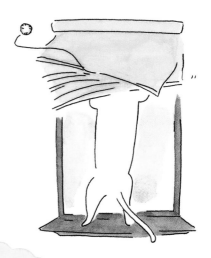

CHASE
THE BUTTERFLIES.

INVESTIGATE THE SHADOWS.

MAKE YOUR OWN HOURS.

SHRED ALL DOCUMENTS.

MONEY'S ONLY PAPER.

BE CURIOUS.

GET TO KNOW PEOPLE IN HIGH PLACES.

DON'T BE AFRAID TO TAKE CHANCES.

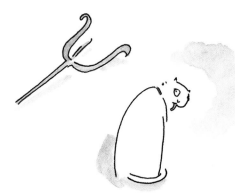

TAKE A MOMENT
TO RECOVER YOUR DIGNITY.

BUT DON'T DWELL
TOO MUCH ON THE PAST.

DON'T ALWAYS COME WHEN YOU'RE CALLED.

TRY NEW THINGS.

Gloat.

TAKE SOME TIME TO EAT THE FLOWERS.

STARE UNABASHEDLY.

TEST LIMITS.

BE TOLERANT — BUT NOT OVERLY ACCOMMODATING.

GET MAD WHEN YOU'RE STEPPED ON.

FORGET THAT YOU WERE STEPPED ON.

KNOW ALL THE SUNNY PLACES.

SOMETIMES YOU CAN'T EXPLAIN YOURSELF.

SOMETIMES YOU CAN'T EXPLAIN YOUR ACTIONS.

HAVE A SNEEZE THAT'S THE ENVY OF OTHERS.

CHALLENGE YOURSELF.

SHARE YOUR VICTORIES.

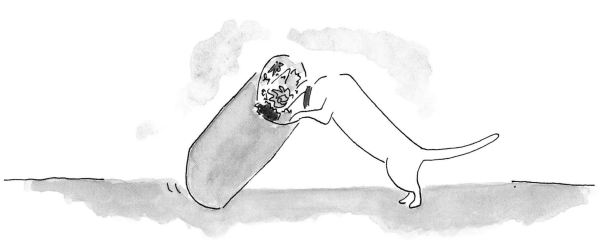

RECYCLE.

EXERCISE DAILY.

SEE A DOCTOR ONCE A YEAR.

PRETEND YOU'VE NEVER HEARD OF FLOSSING.

GO BAREFOOT.

OBEY YOUR INSTINCTS.

CLAIM YOUR OWN CHAIR.

FLAUNT YOUR HAIR LOSS.

TAKE PRIDE IN YOUR WHISKERS.

DON'T PLUCK YOUR EYEBROWS.

VARY YOUR HANGOUTS.

MAKE THE WORLD YOUR PLAYGROUND.

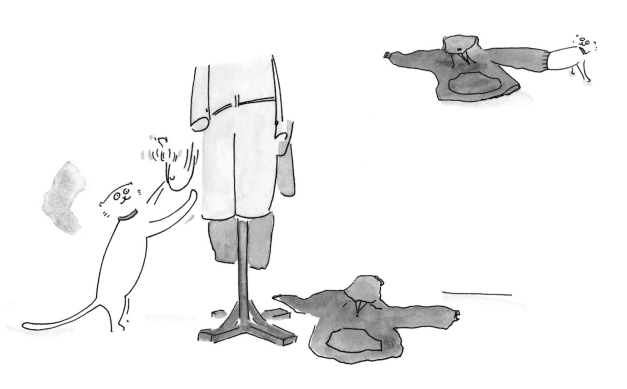

RECOGNIZE THE TOY IN EVERYTHING.

MAKE THE MOST OF UNSTRUCTURED TIME.

THERE IS ALWAYS TIME FOR A NAP.

BE EASY TO COME HOME TO.

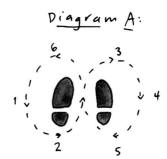

SHOW AFFECTION,

AND CONTENTMENT.

HELP PUT THE GROCERIES AWAY.

EVERYONE IS ENTITLED TO AN OCCASIONAL MOOD SWING.

THE FASTER YOU RUN UPSTAIRS
THE MORE LIKELY YOU ARE TO FORGET WHY YOU WENT
IN THE FIRST PLACE.

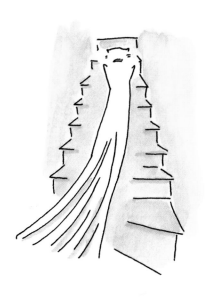

THERE IS NOTHING WRONG WITH CHANGING YOUR MIND.

Time
elapsed    0 : 0 0          0 : 0 2          0 : 0 2 ½          0 : 0 3
(seconds)

AVOID COMPANY YOU DO NOT LIKE.

ACCEPT THAT NOT ALL COMPANY WILL LIKE YOU.

LOVE UNCONDITIONALLY.

DEPEND ON OTHERS WITHOUT LOSING YOUR INDEPENDENCE.

ENJOY YOUR OWN COMPANY.

BE A GOOD LISTENER.

INVITE YOURSELF TO DINNER.

SCRATCH WHEN IT ITCHES.

Don't drool.

GET USED TO SILENCES.

BE ENTERTAINING.

STRIKE POSES.

1.　　　　2.　　　　3.

W I G G L E   Y O U R   E A R S .

JUMP RIGHT INTO THE MIDDLE OF THINGS.

JUST BECAUSE YOU'RE HOME,
YOU DON'T HAVE TO ANSWER THE PHONE.

FEEL NO GUILT.

Use negative attention-getting ONLY as a last resort.

ASK FOR ATTENTION.

IGNORE T.V.

YAWN LIKE YOU MEAN IT.

FIND A GOOD LAP TO CURL UP IN.

BE SOFT.

BE COOL.

BE MYSTERIOUS.

BE ABLE TO MAKE
SOMEONE FEEL BETTER
BY JUST BEING THERE.

Walk softly.

MAKE PEOPLE WONDER WHAT YOU DO AT NIGHT.

BE GOOD AT FINDING THINGS IN THE DARK.

HAVE A WARM BED.

BE LOVED.

DREAM.

# AND THEN SOME

(The New)

MY CAT

ANY DAY CAN BE THE BEGINNING OF A NEW YEAR.

DON'T DRAG OUT
GOOD-BYES.

PEOPLE
WATCHING
IS A
LEGITIMATE
PASTIME.

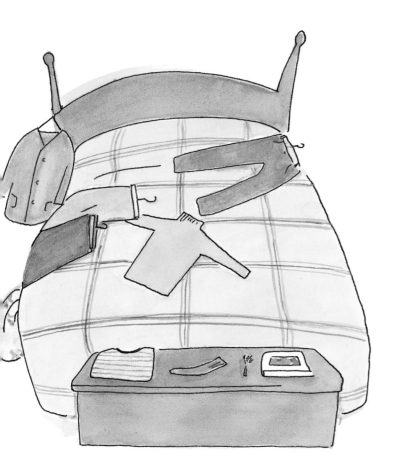

ASK FOR HELP

WHEN YOU NEED IT.

DON'T TAKE "NO" FOR AN ANSWER.

COMPROMISES AREN'T ALL BAD.

BE A
CALMING
INFLUENCE.

HAVE A GOOD INDOOR
EXERCISE PROGRAM.

A

BE FLEXIBLE.

BE GRACEFUL.

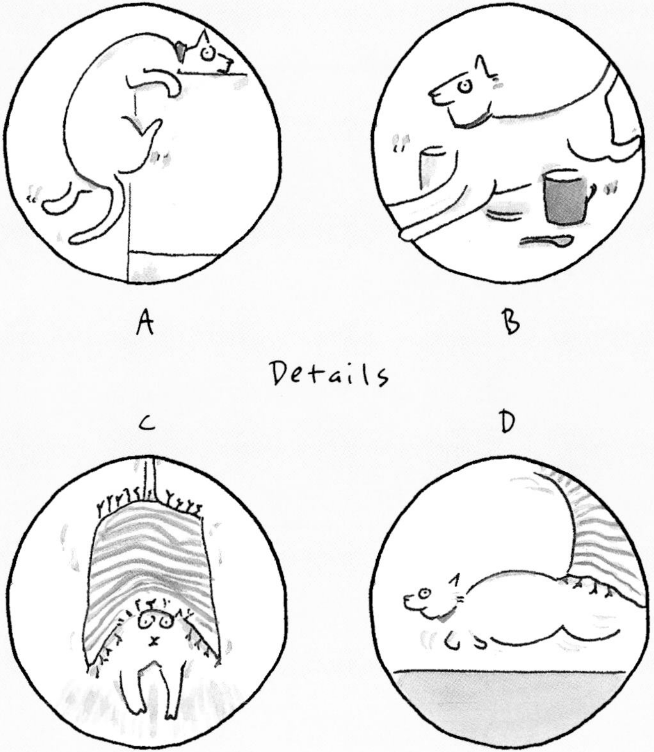

A

B

Details

C

D

BE CREATIVE.

BE YOURSELF.

DON'T THINK TOO FAR BEYOND YOUR NEXT MEAL.

BE ABLE TO NAP ANYWHERE.

HAVE A YEN FOR THE GREAT OUTDOORS.

COMMUNE
WITH THE
BIRDS.

CELEBRATE DAYS WHEN
YOU CAN OPEN THE WINDOWS.

BE PATIENT.                              THINK BIG.

KNOW WHEN
TO FIGHT
AND WHEN
TO RUN.

DON'T HOLD BACK.

THERE IS MORE THAN ONE WAY
TO SHOW AFFECTION.

YOU CAN NEVER SAY
"I LOVE YOU"
TOO MANY TIMES.

RESIST BEING PUT IN BOXES.

HAVE A PLACE WHERE NO ONE CAN FIND YOU.

Cross section:

AIR YOUR GRIEVANCES.

MAKE THE MOST OF YOUR PRIVATE TIME.

Time elapsed :10

:59

:20

1:30

"Lord of the Box"

2:03

SET LIMITS.

ENFORCE THEM.

Reminder:

IF YOU DON'T COOK,
HELP WITH THE DISHES.

THE BEST WATER
DOESN'T COME IN FANCY BOTTLES.

BE MISCHIEVOUS.

DON'T BETRAY CONFIDENCES.

THERE IS SOMETHING ABOUT WARM LAUNDRY.

BE ABLE TO SIT AND DO NOTHING.

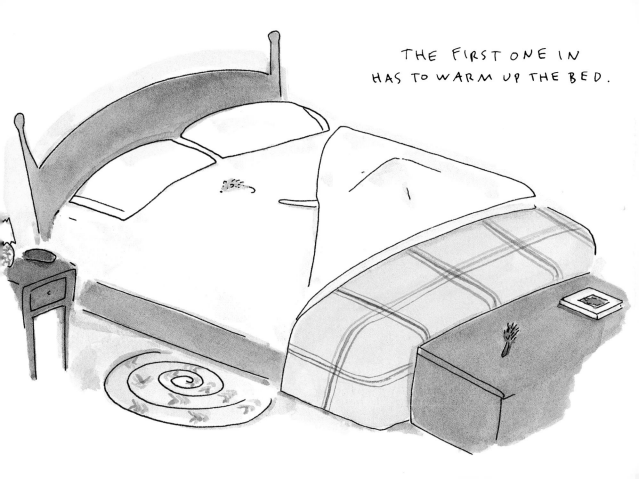

DON'T HOG THE BLANKETS.

SHARE
THE PILLOWS.

YOU CAN ALWAYS MAKE ROOM FOR ONE MORE.

TAKE A WALK UNDER A FULL MOON.

RECOGNIZE
THE SHADOWS.

FALL BACK TO SLEEP EASILY.

DREAM NEW DREAMS.